Fix your Phonics

Workbook Grade 1

OM KIDZ
An imprint of Om Books International

AMAZING ALPHABET

Suki the Starfish wants to learn new words. Fill in the blanks to complete the words and recite them aloud to help her learn.

A __ __ L __

F __ S __

J __ __ L __

B __ L __

G __ __ S __

K __ __ E

C __ __ B

H __ R __

L __ O __

D __ __ PH __ __

I __ K

__ A __

N__T

__A__

W__ __E__

O__ __O__ __S

S__A__L

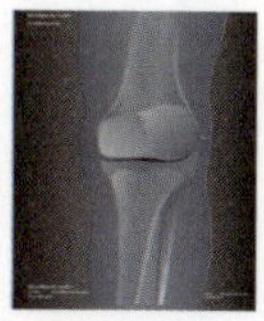

__-R__Y

P__ __A__E

__ __G__R

__A__ __T

__ __EE__

U__ __C__ __N

Z__ __R__

LETTER LAKE

Help Frodo the Frog pull out the vowels from the letter lake.

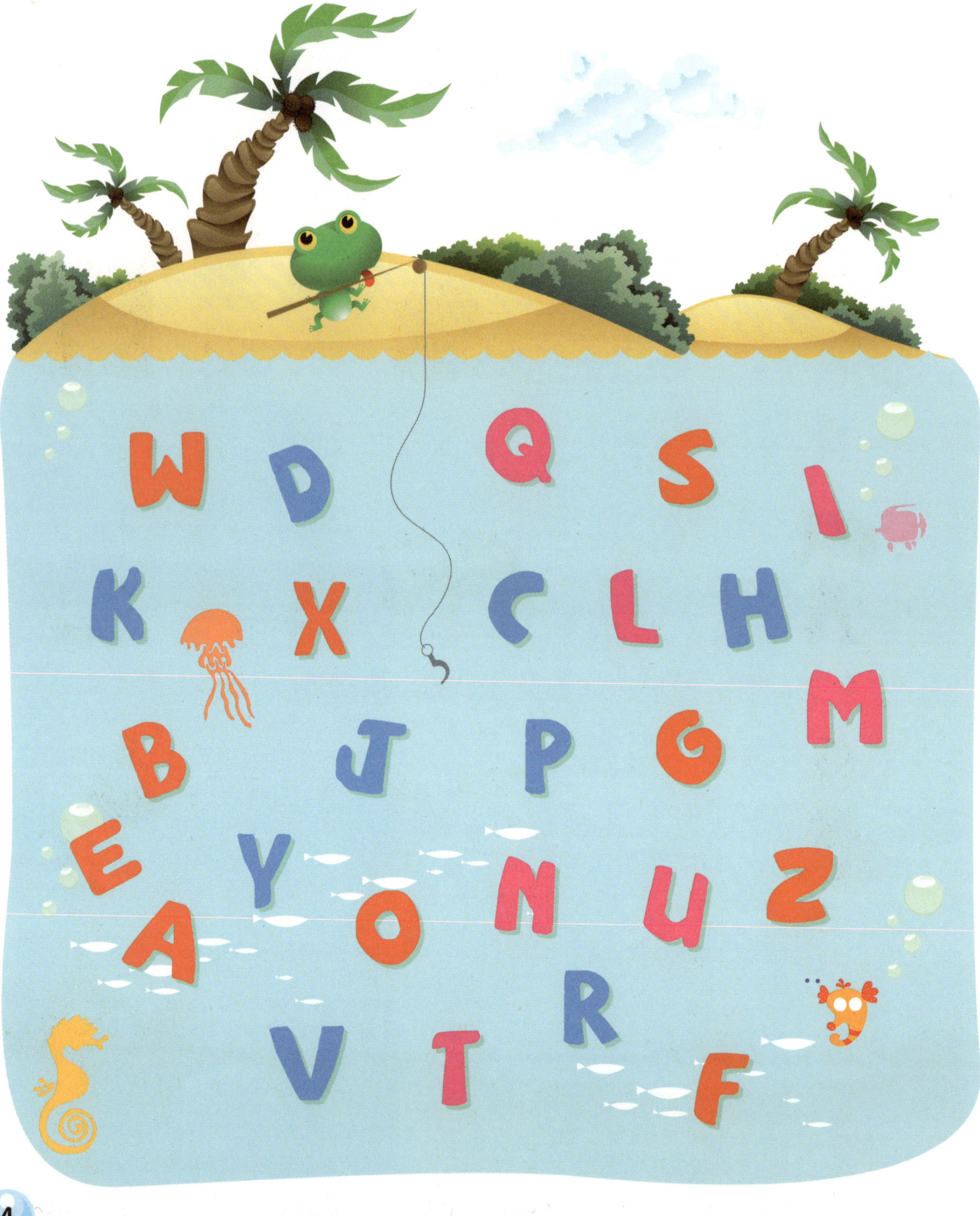

TROUBLING TWO

Phil the Fish can't seem to find two-letter words. Can you find and circle them in the grid below? Look at the seashells for clues.

b	l	e	r	p	i	n	g
e	q	a	j	o	f	r	u
i	w	t	u	m	l	o	r
m	o	f	a	n	a	s	p
n	n	o	m	p	g	n	g
i	t	l	i	s	x	s	o
h	e	k	b	m	e	n	b
g	p	u	s	i	d	g	l

OCTOJUMBLE

Olga the Octopus was learning about the 'a' family when she jumbled it all up! Rearrange the letters to form words from the 'a' family.

d b a ________

a d s ________

m d a ________

a d l ________

c t a ________

t b a ________

a t f ________

t r a ________

nam ______

fna ______

nap ______

pca ______

spa ______

pta ______

amd ______

mar ______

PERFECT MATCH

Help Stevie the Stingray learn more about the 'a' family by matching the pictures to their names. Don't forget to read the names aloud!

bear

lair

mare

stair

hare

MONSTER MAZE

Help Phil the Fish reach his food by tracing a path through the maze. Follow the path with words from the 'a' family.

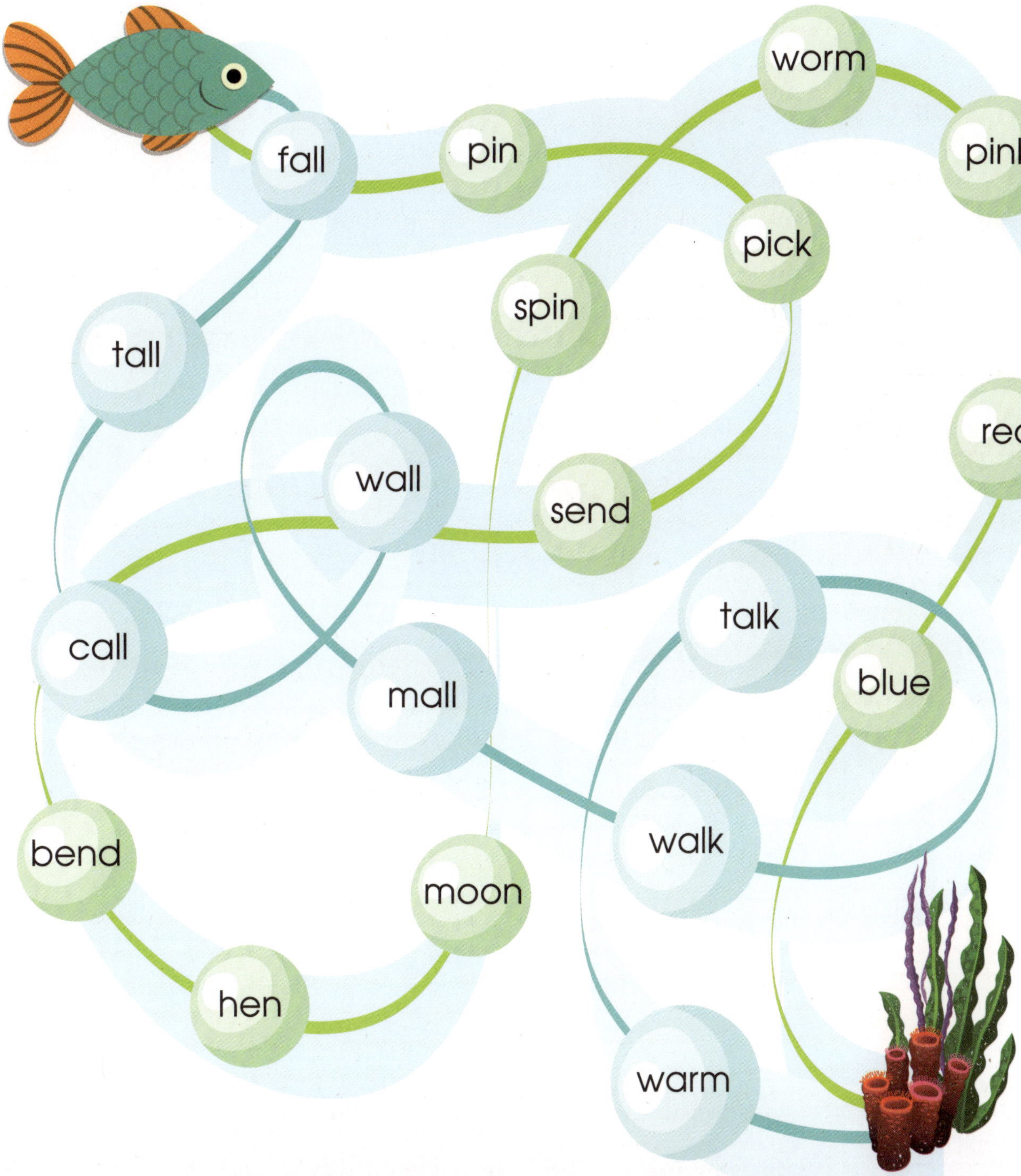

WORD BUILDER

Look at the words in the first picture. Change just the first letter and form new words to make the underwater path.

Pail	Take	Late	Day
________	________	________	________
________	________	________	________
________	________	________	________
________	________	________	________

WORD ALERT

Fish out the bottles by circling the ones with 'a' words in them.

TANGLED WORDS

Untangle the ropes and connect the pictures to their correct word corals.

EDDIE'S E-WORDS

Help Eddie the Eel learn about 'e' words by filling the blanks.

A fish got caught in the fisherman's ____________.

Five and five sum up to ____________.

A man can run on his two ____________.

A lion lives in a ____________.

Hidden in an oyster is a precious ____________.

Can you write with a ____________?

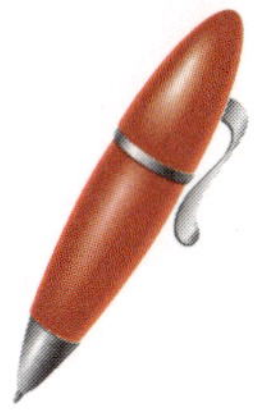

FISHY TROUBLE

Colour the fish whose words share the same 'e' sound as 'feet'. Cross out the rest.

heed
creep
weep
deep
man
pan
fan
land
lone
stone
punk
rust

UNDERWATER CROSSWORD

Look at the pictures and solve the clues to complete the crossword.

Across

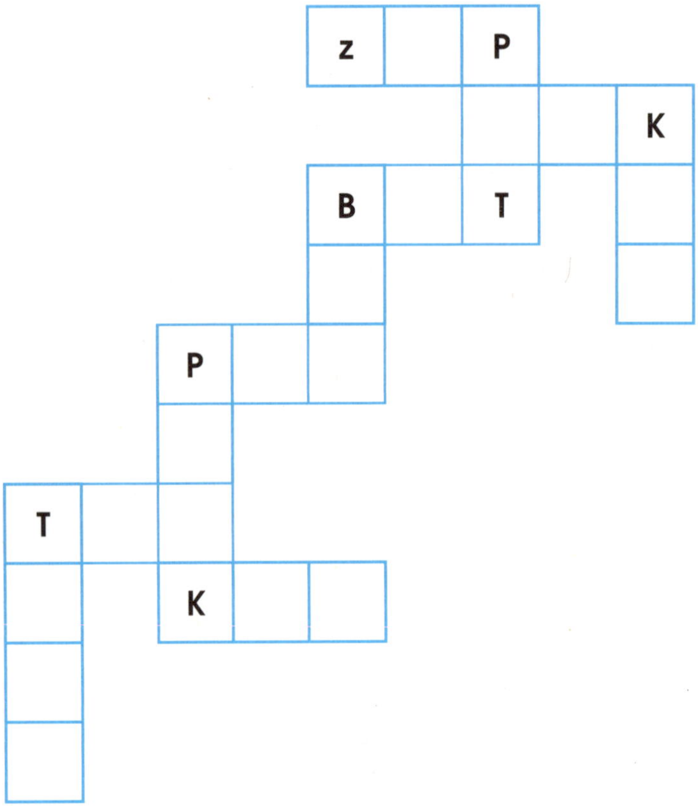

Down

SHIP SEARCH

Look at the words below and circle the ones belonging to the 'i' family.

PERFECT MATCH

Help Kiki the Clownfish match these pictures to the correct 'i' words.

lime

bike

kite

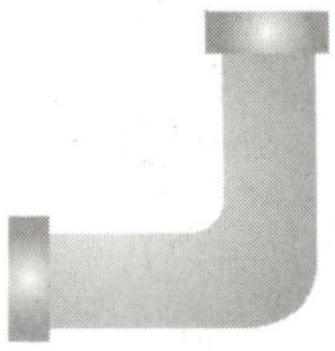

five

pipe

smile

UNDER THE SEA

Read Willie the Whale's poem and circle the words that share the same 'i' sound as 'dive'.

The blue sea is so big and fine
With cool fish who are my friends of mine.

Swimmers come in for a dive
In groups of two and three and five.

The fish in the sea are so very wise
If you'd meet them, you'd give them a prize.

Come swim with us, we'll give you a ride
And let you surf the evening tide.

WATERY JUMBLE

Fish out the letters from the oysters and make as many three letter words as you can. Remember, all of them must have the letter 'o'.

SHARK ATTACK

Help Fifi the Fish escape from the Scary Shark! Follow the path with 'o' words to find your way out of the maze.

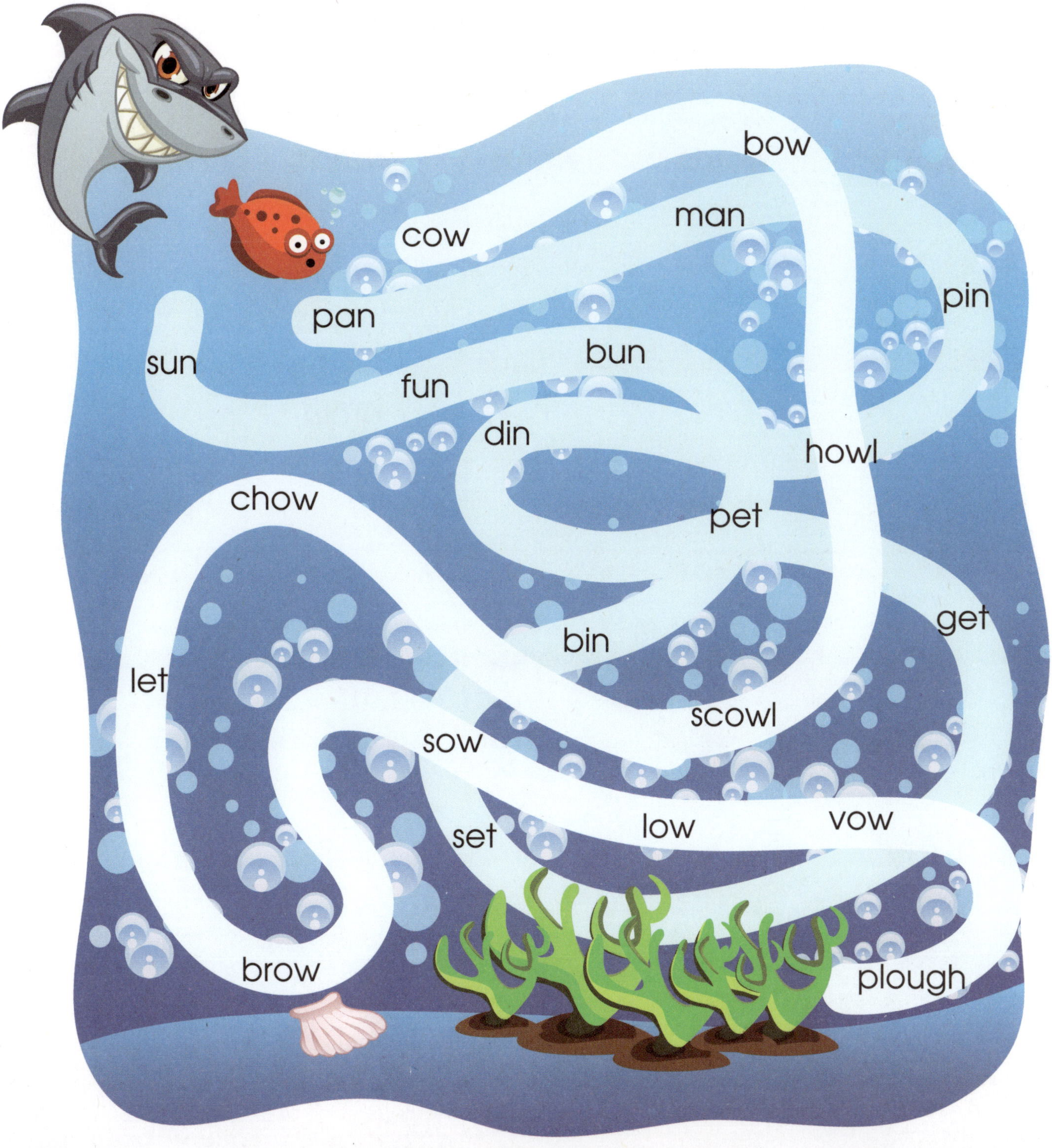

WORD TABLE

Swishy the Swordfish is making a table of 'o' words. Help him fill up the tables by following the examples below.

'-ope' words	'-one' words	'-oad' words	'-ow' words	'-ose' words
		toad		
rope				
			grow	
	drone			prose

SEA SORTING

Sandy the Starfish is sorting her words. Draw lines and connect the words to the correct word families at the bottom.

RIVER RUN

The fish have lined up for a river run. Find out which fish won by connecting the leaves with rhyming words.

WORDHUNT

Find and circle the 'u' words on the water board below.

rat

dot

rub sit

sum

gut cut

tub

jug hate

jut

hat

bug smug

but bud

hum got

cup

FISHY FILLERS

Help the fish name these pictures by filling the blanks.

t __ __ e

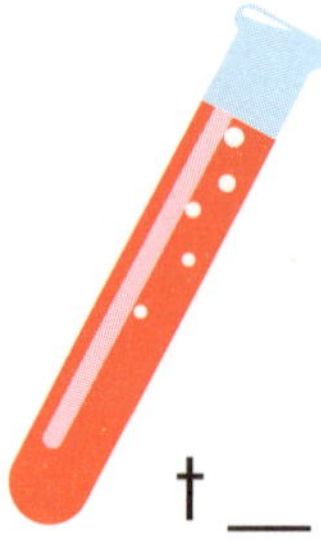

t __ b __

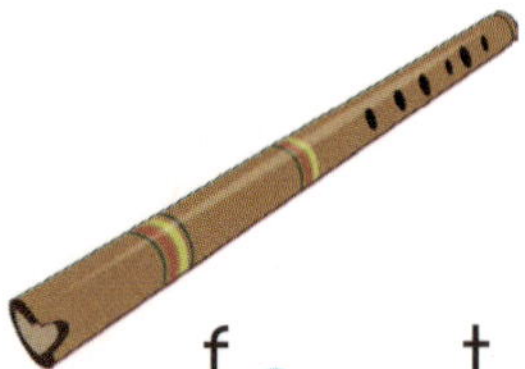

f __ __ t __

m __ l __

__ u __ c __

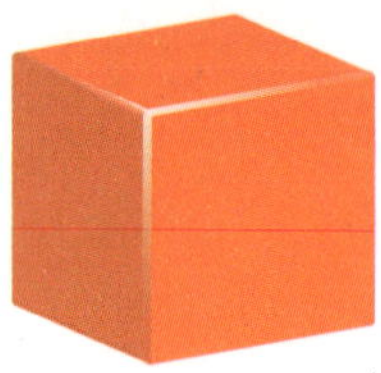

__ u __ e

UNDERWATER SCRAMBLE

Unscramble the letters to form words belonging to the 'u' family.

n t u e

s e u

l g e u

n r e p u

l b e u

e u t r

t u s i

l u e r

c t e u

n d e u

RHYMING MATCH

Help Jojo the Jellyfish match the rhyming words on this page.

sore	trip
cube	lore
mile	tram
feed	pail
sail	need
scam	pile
drip	tube

SENTENCE SPOTTER

Help Hagger the Hippo teach his fishy friends some rhymes! Circle the rhyming words in each sentence.

I looked at the map and took a nap.

This gel looks swell on my hair.

I went for a jog and met a talking frog.

I like to hum when I work on a sum.

I walked a mile and it took me a while.

My dog likes to sit on a log.

FISHY FRIENDS

Sing the poem and circle the rhyming words in it.

My fish friends live in the blue sea
Come to meet them, swim with me.

That over there is the great white shark
His voice is louder than a dog's bark.

Those big giants are the big blue whales
They are good at telling funny tales.

That's the octopus, with eight big legs
On which he juggles barrels and kegs.

The sea is so vast and full of fun
There's something good for everyone.

ANSWERS

Page 2

Page 3

Page 4

Page 5

b	l	e	r	p	i	n	g
e	q	a	j	o	f	r	u
i	w	t	u	m	l	o	r
m	o	f	a	n	a	s	p
n	n	o	m	p	g	n	g
i	t	l	i	s	x	s	o
h	e	k	b	m	e	n	b
g	p	u	s	i	d	g	l

Page 6

Page 7

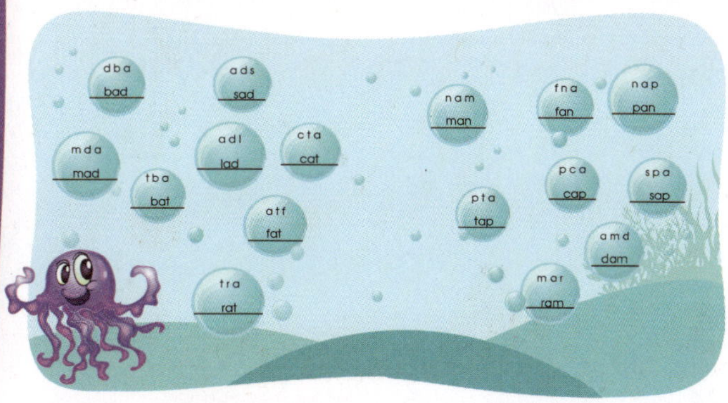

Page 8

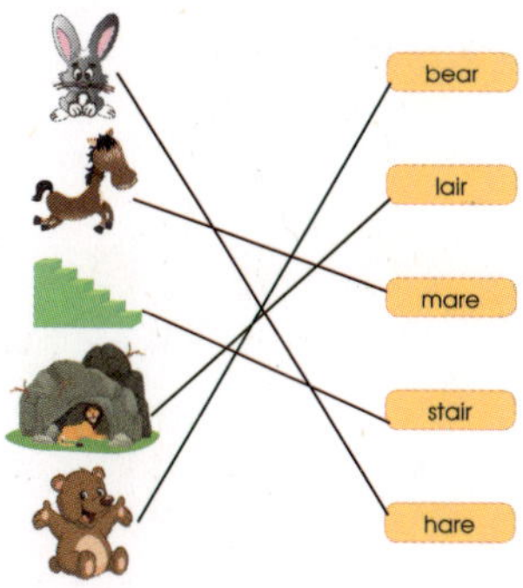

Page 9

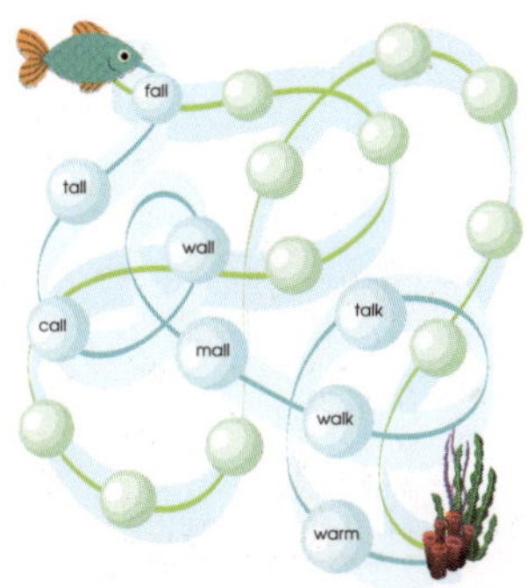

Page 10

Pail	Take	Late	Day
Mail	Make	Mate	Hay
Tail	Lake	Date	Bay
Sail	Bake	Hate	Lay
Nail	Sake	Rate	Say

Page 11

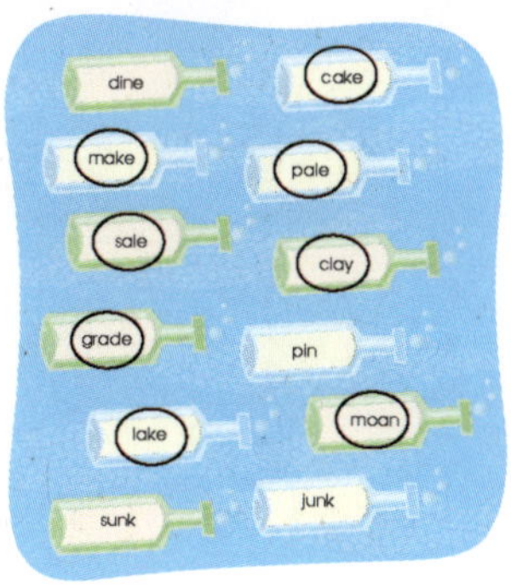

Page 12

bed

red

ten

men

hen

jet

Page 13

A fish got caught in the fisherman's net.

Five and five sum up to ten.

A man can run on his two legs.

A lion lives in a den.

Hidden in an oyster is a precious gem.

Can you write with a pen?

Pages 14-15

sheet	feed
meet	need
greet	heed
week	weep
peek	creep
meek	deep

Page 16

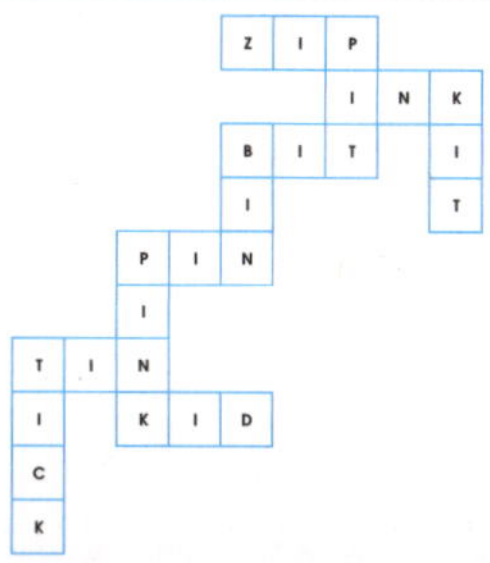

Page 17

Page 18

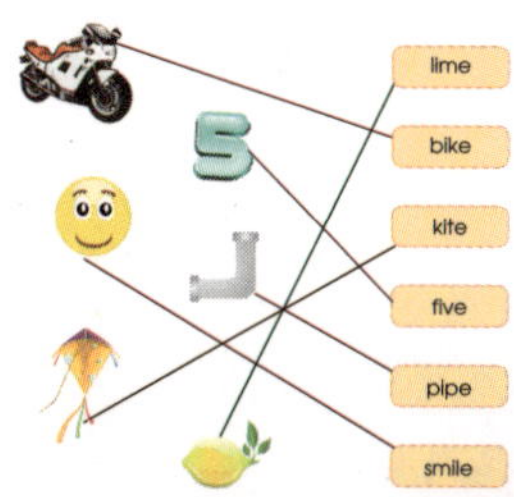

ANSWERS

Page 19

The blue sea is so big and fine
With cool fish who are my friends of mine
Swimmers come in for a dive
In groups of two and three and five
The fish in the sea are so very wise
If you'd meet them, you'd give them a prize
Come swim with us, we'll give you a ride
And let you surf the evening tide

Page 20

Page 21

Page 22

'-ope' words	'-one' words	'-oad' words	'-ow' words	'-ose' words
cope	lone	toad	mow	rose
rope	tone	goad	sow	pose
mope	stone	load	grow	dose
hope	drone	road	tow	prose

Page 23

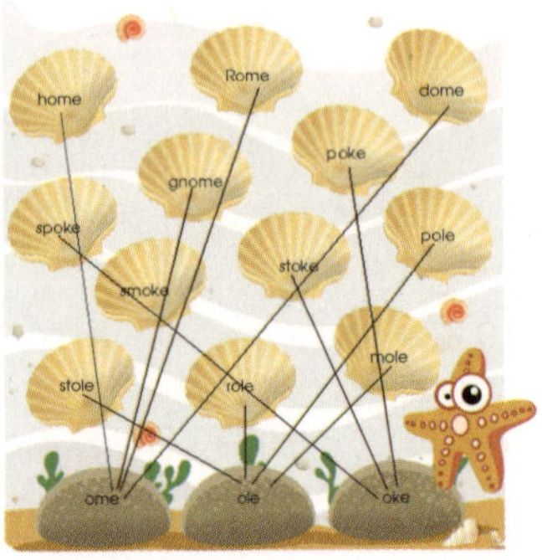

Page 24

Page 25

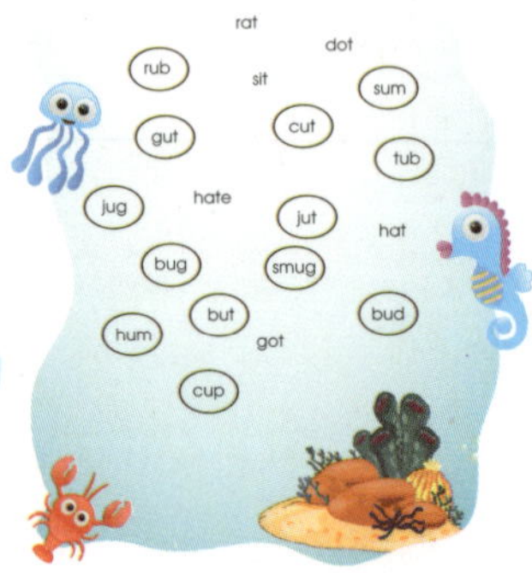

Page 26

Page 27

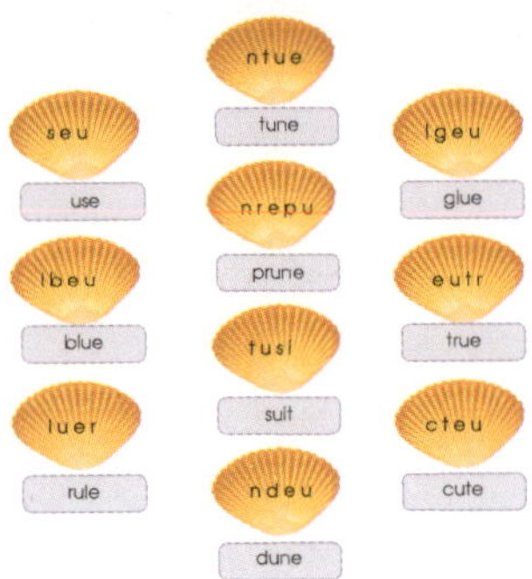

Page 28

Page 29

I looked at the map and took a nap.
This gel looks swell on my hair.
I went for a jog and met a talking frog.
I like to hum when I work on a sum.
I walked a mile and it took me a while.
My dog likes to sit on a log.

Page 30

My fish friends live in the blue sea
Come to meet them, swim with me.

That over there is the great white shark
His voice is louder than a dog's bark.

Those big giants are the big blue whales
They are good at telling funny tales.

That's the octopus, with eight big legs
On which he juggles barrels and kegs.

The sea is so vast and full of fun
There's something good for everyone.